Martial Arts

Bernie Blackall

Special thanks to Tom Sommerville, Bill Cullen's Karate, for his assistance during the production of this book.

Heinemann Library
Des Plaines, Illinois

First published in the United States by Heinemann Library,
an imprint of Reed Educational & Professional Publishing,
1350 East Touhy Avenue, Suite 240 West
Des Plaines, IL 60018

03 02 01 00 99
10 9 8 7 6 5 4 3 2 1

The publisher would like to thank Anthony Steele and Andreina Santiago for their assistance.

Series cover and text design by Karen Young
Paged by Jo Pritchard
Cover by Smarty-pants Design
Cover photographs by Mike Liles
Edited by Jane Pearson
Illustrations by Vasja Koman
Picture research by Kirsty Grant and Lara Artis
Production by Cindy Smith
Film separations by Impact Printing Pty Ltd
Printed in Hong Kong by Wing King Tong

Library of Congress Cataloging-in-Publication Data
Blackall, Bernie, 1956-
      Martial Arts/Bernie Blackall
          p.   m. -- (Top sport)
      Includes bibliographical references (p.) and index.
      Summary: Introduces the martial arts, discussing their history, American highlights, equipment, rules, and various forms, inlcuding judo, karate, and aikido.
      ISBN 1-57572-705-6 (lib. bdg.)
      1. Martial arts--Juvenile literature.   [1. Martial arts.]
      I. Title. II. Series: Blackall, Bernie, 1956-   Top sport.
      GV1101.B53 1998
      796.8--dc21   98-19590
                                                        CIP
                                                         AC

Photographs supplied by:
Coo-ee Picture Library: p. 23. Michael Egan pp. 10, 24, 25, 26. Mike Liles: pp. 8, 11, 14. Sport. The Library: Andrew Freeman, pp. 5, 15, 16; Darren McNamara, p. 21; Presse Sports, p. 13. Sydney Freelance: p. 19. Doug Churchill Photography/Black Belt Magazine, p. 6, 7;

Martial arts require specialist instruction. Do not attempt any of the techniques and movements in this book without a qualified, registered instructor present.

Contents

About Martial Arts

There are many different forms of martial arts including aikido, judo, karate, ju-jitsu, kempo, tai chi chuan, kung fu, tae kwon do, and Thai kick boxing. The term "martial arts" means arts concerned with the waging of war. Most of the martial arts known today were developed from ancient war skills.

The martial arts originated in Asia. They are shrouded in tradition and mystery. Each country (and even in some cases each region) developed its own fighting skills. A process of trial and error ensured that these "arts" were refined and honed to perfection.

Rules developed over many years to control martial arts. They ensured that contestants had equal chances of winning and helped to reduce the risk of serious injury (or even death). Rules also standardized the way contests were conducted throughout the world.

Today the overall aim of the martial arts is for participants to develop physical fitness and mental discipline through the learning of defensive combat techniques. This book focuses on three martial arts:

• karate—which consists of striking, kicking, and punching moves

• judo—which consists of throwing and grappling moves

• aikido—which consists of self-defense and redirecting force moves.

The language of the martial arts

Many official martial arts terms are Japanese, Korean, or Chinese. You don't need to learn a new language to participate in martial arts, but it is important that you learn the names for the techniques and the refereeing terms. The terms you will need to know are explained throughout the book and also appear in the glossary.

Kicking is one of the many moves in karate.

Origins of the martial arts
• Japan–aikido, judo, ju-jitsu, karate, kempo
• China–kung fu, tai chi chuan
• Korea–tae kwon do
• Thailand–Thai kick boxing

U.S. Highlights

Martial Arts are a relative newcomer to the United States. During World War II U.S. soldiers stationed in Okinawa learned karate. When they returned home in 1948, they brought karate with them.

In the years since, the popularity of karate and martial arts has skyrocketed. In any town or city one can find martial arts training of some variety. Like many sports, people learn martial arts for different reasons—from increasing athletic ability, to defense, to training a peaceful mind. Both men and women are active in martial arts. There are many different levels of competition from informal competitions to national and international events.

In the U.S., Joe Lewis has had the most impact on the sport. His training began in Okinawa and his career spanned more than seventeen years. He won more titles, set more records, and instituted more innovations than anyone else in the history of karate. His greatest

Herb Perez

honor came in 1985 when a Karate Illustrated survey chose him as "The greatest Karate Fighter of All Time."

Herb Perez

Herb Perez is another outstanding martial arts athlete. He was twelve years old when he walked into a martial arts school and discovered his passion. In 1983, at age 23, he competed in his first National Tae kwon do Championship and two years later he won the bronze medal. At age 32, he was a gold medalist in the middleweight competition in tae kwon do at the 1992 Olympic games, the first Olympic games he participated in. He has been a champion and leader in the martial arts for many years. He is a six-time National Team Captain and a three-time winner of the Pan American Championship. In 1988 he was inducted into the Tae Kwon do Hall of fame. Other gold medals include Pan American Tae kwon do Championship in 1989, 1987, and 1986; the World Cup Championship, and the Pan American Games.

Kathy Long

Kathy Long has a long list of accomplishments in martial arts. Her career began in 1980 at the age of 15 when she began to study aikido. She learned kung fu, boxing, kickboxing, and shoinryo karate. In kickboxing she holds two world titles from the Karate International Coucil of Kickboxing (KICK), one world title from the World Karate Association, a world title from International Sport Karate (ISKA) in 1991, and one from World Martial Arts Challenge

Association. She was indoctrinated as the female of the year into the Blackbelt Hall of Fame in 1992 and the Kung Fu Hall of Fame. Along with performing, she is an author and actress, appearing on television shows such as Walker Texas Ranger.

Kathy Long

What You Need

Martial arts clothing

The martial arts suit is called a **judogi** in judo and aikido and a **gi** in karate. It consists of a white jacket and pants made from heavy cotton fabric that can withstand a lot of tugging. Female participants may wear a T-shirt or swimsuit under the suit.

Both boys and girls close the jacket left over right. It should be big enough to overlap by about 8 inches (20 centimeters). The **belt** is used to hold the jacket in place. It must be long enough to go around your waist twice with enough left to tie a square knot with 8 to 12 inches (20 to 30 centimeters) left hanging. The color of your belt is a special source of pride in the martial arts as it tells others what grade you have reached. The pants are kept up with a drawstring and their correct length is about 2 inches (5 centimeters) above the ankle joint.

It is important to take good care of the martial arts suit and to wash it after each training session.

The martial arts kit

The martial arts suit is made from a heavy cotton fabric that can withstand tugging.

Safety

- Do not wear watches or jewelry.
- Keep fingernails and toenails trimmed short.
- Tie long hair back, but never with metal clips.
- Footwear, of any type, must not be worn on the mat.

How to tie your belt

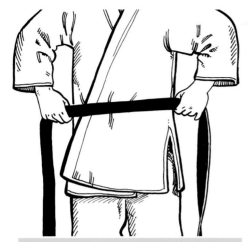

1. Keeping the two ends equal, wrap the belt around your waist, across your stomach first.

2. Cross the ends over at the back and bring them back to the front.

3. Cross the left end over the right. Pull it up behind both layers of the belt.

4. Now tie the free ends together right over left and pull them through to finish the knot.

Some martial arts terms

In any martial arts technique or move there is a winner and a loser. In judo the **tori** is the winner of the move, and the **uke** is the loser. A contest is made up of many moves, and the competitors each become the tori and the uke, depending on how successfully they attack and defend each move. If one contestant attacks successfully, he or she will be the tori for that move. If the attack is successfully defended with a counterattack, then the foiled attacker is the uke and the counterattacker is the tori. In aikido, the winner is called **nage** and the loser, uke. The same terms are used for practice in the school (**dojo**).

The Playing Area

The room where martial arts competitions and practices take place is called a **dojo**.

The judo and aikido competition area is 26 to 33 feet (8 to 10 meters) square, surrounded by a 3-foot (1-meter)wide red danger area. The karate area is 26 feet (8 meters) square with a surrounding 3-foot-wide safety area which is part of the playing area, and you may not step outside it. The area is cushioned with mats about 2.0 inches(50 millimeters) thick, although karate classes do not always use mats.

Rules of the dojo

There are certain rules and guidelines for the dojo, regardless of which martial art you are practicing. The dojo rules date back to the original Japanese traditions—they help the instructor teach the student and the student learn the skills of martial arts.

Observe the following rules when practicing in the dojo:

- Never bully less skillful or weaker people than yourself.

The martial arts action takes place on mats in the dojo.

- Always wear footwear between the change rooms and the mat to keep your feet clean before you begin practice.

- Never use martial arts outside the dojo—unless as a last resort in self-defense.

- Bow when you enter and leave the dojo. This lets the instructor know that you are ready to start. It is also a sign of respect to the martial arts.

- When training or competing, keep a cool head—control your emotions. Tantrums or angry, impulsive behavior will cause lapses in concentration, allowing your opponent to gain the upper hand.

- The dojo is an area of order and control. Listen very carefully to your instructor.

Bowing

Bowing is an Asian greeting and a way of showing respect. In the dojo you bow to show respect to your teacher and to your opponents.

Bow when you enter or leave the dojo or before and after each contest. This indicates to the instructor you are ready to start or to leave.

Bowing to your opponent at the start of a contest tells your opponent you are ready to begin.

Bowing at the end of a training session or contest is a traditional mark of respect for your opponent and your instructor.

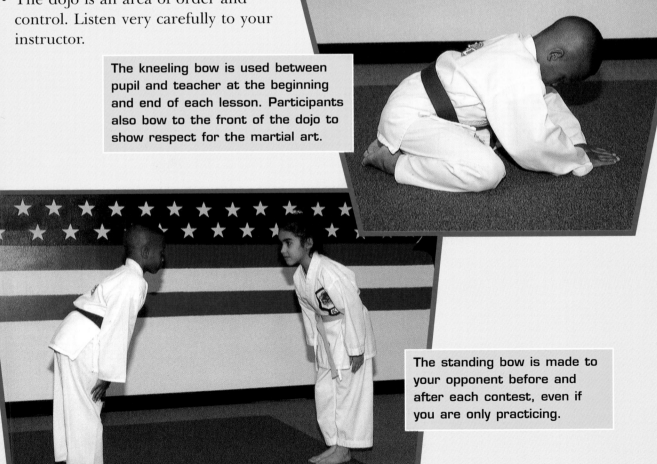

The kneeling bow is used between pupil and teacher at the beginning and end of each lesson. Participants also bow to the front of the dojo to show respect for the martial art.

The standing bow is made to your opponent before and after each contest, even if you are only practicing.

Karate

Karate consists of a series of **blocks** and counterblocks using the hands and feet. The word karate means "empty hand" in Japanese. This form of combat gets its name because it involves no weapons—the hands are empty. However, all parts of the body are used as weapons in karate.

History

Karate developed from the art of Chinese boxing (kempo). It was very popular on the island of Okinawa, then part of China. In 1609 Okinawa was conquered by the Japanese, who banned all martial arts. But kempo survived and later developed into karate. In 1922 Ginchin Funakoshi demonstrated karate on the main islands of Japan where it went on to become very popular.

During World War II, Okinawa was occupied by several American military bases. Many servicemen became so skilled and dedicated to karate that on their return to the United States they opened karate schools.

Since World War II, karate has grown at a tremendous rate. The World Union of Karate Organizations was formed in 1970 to govern and promote karate. The World Karate Federation now has more than 150 member nations.

The contest

The karate competition area is 17x17 feet (8x8 meters). Two starting lines, 13 feet (4 meters) apart, are marked on the center of the match area. The contest begins with each contestant standing behind the starting line. They bow to one another. The referee calls "shobu sanbon hajime," and the karate match begins. The match lasts 2 minutes for juniors and women, and 3 minutes for men. The match may be extended to 5 minutes when a result is not achieved.

One referee controls the contest from the center of the match area. He is responsible for starting and finishing the contest, for awarding points, giving warnings, and awarding fouls. The referee is assisted by four corner judges.

Junior karate grades

Progress in karate is measured through a grading system. Each grade is called a **kyu**.

The kyu are each identified with a colored belt. The early grades teach proficiency in the basic moves. The higher grades concentrate on learning how to use the moves.

Only three colored belts were used originally—white, green, and brown—but other colors have been added. A typical sequence is white, yellow, orange, green, purple, brown, black.

Scoring zone

The **karateka** (karate player) scores by using legal techniques on specific areas of his or her opponent's body.

As blows delivered with force and speed are very dangerous, karateka "pull" their blows—the full force of a punch or kick is concentrated on an area just in front of the opponent's target area. The referee will allow no contact at all to the head and face, and only light blows to the body. Excessive physical contact results in disqualification.

The dark shaded areas are the target areas.

Winning the competition

There are two kinds of points scored in a top karate match: an **ippon** is a full point and a **waza ari** is a half point. One ippon is scored for a vigorous blow to the target area that demonstrates good timing and technique. It is also awarded for certain blow combinations, for an attack on an undefended target, and when an opponent moves forward to receive a weaker blow, or when he loses balance. A waza ari is scored when a blow is slightly flawed in technique. Points are registered only for techniques that are cleanly performed and directed strongly at the target areas.

To win a match, the karateka must score three ippons. If neither contestant scores three ippons, the match is awarded to the karateka with the most points.

Penalties

When a karateka infringes with a dangerous move, the referee will warn or penalize him or her. Warnings are given for minor infringements. If the infraction occurs again, the opponent is awarded a waza ari (half point).

This kick is outside the scoring zone so will not score a point.

Karate

Walking stance

The stances

There are four positions that can form the basis of all karate techniques—the **yoi stance**, the walking stance, the forward stance, and the back stance.

Yoi stance

Take a half pace forward from the yoi position. Bring your shoulder and hip slightly forward with your leading leg. The walking stance allows for a rapid change in direction.

Forward stance

From the yoi stance, or ready position, you are ready to move into other positions. Stand with your feet about shoulder-width apart and your fists clenched in front of you.

From the walking stance, advance a further half step with your lead leg. Your leading hip and shoulder should move forward, too, so that your body is facing just to the side of your opponent. Your feet should be parallel and pointing directly in front of you and your head should be facing your opponent.

Stand with one leg behind the other. Bend your rear leg so that it supports most of your weight, and hold your shoulders in line with your hips. This stance can be used when your opponent withdraws slightly in preparation for a block or counterattack.

Hand strikes

Karateka are able to score in a competition with kicks or hand strikes to the scoring zone.

Hand strikes are delivered most effectively at high speed, following the shortest possible route.

Lunge punch

The karateka steps forward, and the instant his leading leg touches the ground, he throws the punch. The punch is delivered from the fist on the same side as the leading leg. The power of this punch is generated from the forward movement of the body as the shoulders and hips are thrust forward with the leading leg.

There are three possible hitting zones. Punches to the lower stomach are called **gedan**, those to the mid-section of the body are called **chudan**, and punches to the head are called **jodan**.

Begin the lunge punch with one leg forward and one arm outstretched. Your punching hand is bent at your side. Slide your back leg up and step forward. As you put your foot down, pull back your leading arm and thrust your punching arm forward. Your wrist and arm should be straight as you make contact.

Practice punching as a partner or your teacher holds a focus pad for their protection and also as a target for you to aim for.

Making a fist

In a karate punch, only the first two knuckles are used to strike the target area. It is important to clench your fists correctly in preparation for punching.

1. Stretch open the fingers and palm wide at least ten times.

2. Curl your fingers into your palms and then wrap your thumbs around the outsides of the locked fingers. Imagine that your fingers and thumb have squeezed all the air from your fists.

Karate

Kicking

A kick is a strong move and has greater reach than a punch. A kick is ideal for a smaller **karateka,** who can compensate for his opponent's longer arm reach by using his legs as defensive or offensive weapons.

Front kick

While you are learning this kick, think of it as involving three steps. As your technique improves, you can combine the steps into one smooth action.

Practice kicking as a partner holds a focus pad for protection and as a target for you to aim for.

Start in the forward stance position with your left foot forward.

Back foot forward. Raise it strongly with your knee bent. Turn your hips forward.

Thrust your kicking leg outward. Push hips into the kick and bend toes back, hitting with the ball of your foot. Bring your foot back quickly, returning it to the floor ready for a counterattack.

Side kick

The side kick is used for attacking and defending. Impact is made with the heel and edge of the foot. The thrust of the hip provides the power.

Start with your legs apart and knees bent. Lift your kicking leg up with your knee bent. Thrust your heel and the edge of your foot sideways at your target as you lean away from the kick and bend your supporting leg to keep your balance.

Blocking

A **block** prevents an attacking hand or foot strike from hitting its target and so prevents your opponent from scoring. Efficient blocks deflect an attack and allow you to counterattack quickly.

Downward block

The downward block can be used to deflect a blow aimed at about waist height. From the ready position, the karateka steps forward and raises the leading fist to the opposite shoulder. He or she then thrusts this arm down to the leading knee to deflect the attacking strike.

Side kick

Lean away from your target. Bend your support leg for balance.

Upward block

The upward block is used to deflect an attack to the face or head. The karateka raises the right or left arm as he or she steps forward to block the blow. The blocking hand should rise to about 4 inches (10 centimeters) above eye height. The forearm should be parallel to the chest throughout its upward motion and on a 45 degree angle to deflect the attack. The upward block is used in self-defense but rarely in competition.

Judo

Judo is a Japanese word meaning "gentle way." It calls for great skill, good judgement, and quick wits. It is a one-on-one sport where two players, each known as a **judoka**, fight or wrestle one another. The aim is to trip or throw the opponent and/or to hold him or her down in technical submission. While contests are vigorous, the movements are such that injuries are not likely to occur.

History

Judo was created by Professor Jigoro Kano, a great Japanese educator. Kano established his own judo school in Tokyo in 1882. It came to be known as the Kodokan Institute, and eventually became the world headquarters for judo.

Competitions

The aim of the judoka in competition is to unbalance the opponent. He or she may then throw the opponent to the mat. If a throw is not completely successful, the judoka can attempt to pin the opponent down. This is known as **groundwork**.

Contests for junior players last between 2 and 4 minutes. This is actual playing time—with the clock stopping, for example, when players accidentally go outside the mat area. The clock is restarted when play resumes with both players back in the center of the mat.

Referee and judges

A judo match is judged by three referees. One controls the contest and ensures that it is fought within the rules and that all scores are correctly recorded. He signals scores and penalties to the scorer and time keeper.

Two referees sit diagonally opposite each other on the corners of the mat areas. From these positions they are able to observe the competition, especially at the mat edge. They are able to correct or overrule the referee if they both disagree with a decision.

Scoring

There are four kinds of points in judo. An **ippon** is the highest score. A **waza ari** the next highest; then the **yuko** and the **koka**. At the end of the contest, the judoka with the highest quality score wins; for example, one ippon will beat any number of lesser points.

In general play there are two ways to score points:
1. Throw your opponent onto the mat.
2. Pin your opponent to the ground.
The score awarded will depend on how well you do either of these.

Just as you can add to your score with effective throws and holds, penalty points will be deducted from your score when you break the rules.

One judoka wears a red belt over his or her normal belt, and the other wears a white belt. This is to help the referee tell them apart in a contest.

Sometimes judoka finish with the same score, or no score at all. The contest is then awarded to the player that the referees feel has shown the best technique in his or her attempts at throws and groundwork.

Two waza ari = one ippon

Only waza ari points can be added together to make a higher score. If no ippon is scored, the referee and judges will award the contest to the player with the highest quality score. For example, a player with one yuko will beat a player with 10 kokas.

Junior grades

Martial arts beginners start with a white belt. Students aim to progress through the grade levels (kyu) until they have earned a black belt—the highest level. This requires regular practice and years of training.

There are three junior age groups— under 10, under 13, and under 16. Each age group starts with a white belt. Colored stripes are added as the judoka progress.

Depending on the age level, judoka progress to the next color belt after gaining a number of stripes. The order of the belt colors are white, yellow, orange, green, blue, brown, black. Only senior players can be awarded the black belt.

Judo

The techniques that you learn in your judo classes will help you to attack and defend. There are three broad areas of technique for juniors:

- **breakfalls**
- **throws**
- **groundwork**

Breakfalls

When you are thrown, you must land without hurting yourself. All falls involve use of your arm or arms to take the force out of the impact.

Whenever you are thrown, it is important not to simply hit the mat and stop. You should tuck up, roll on the mat, and slap it with your arms and palms of your hands to take the force out of the fall.

Practicing the breakfalls will build your confidence and remove any fear of being thrown. It is best to practice these breakfalls on your own at first. As your confidence and skills grow, practice them with a partner in a proper throwing situation. When you throw somebody, guide them onto the mat to prevent injury.

Standing backwards breakfall

Stand with your arms out straight in front of you.

As you fall back, bend your knees and tuck your head into your arms.

As you strike the mat, slap down hard with both hands. Arms are at a 45 degree angle. Keep your chin toward your chest to prevent hitting your head.

Breakfall techniques are very important at all levels of judo and other martial arts. They form the basis of safe landings from even the most spectacular throws.

Tip for breakfalls

Most **judoka** (as beginners) find it easier to fall to one particular side. In practice and competition you will be thrown to the left or right, so practice your breakfalls equally on both sides.

Side breakfall

Squat low on the mat with your left leg and your left arm stretched out.

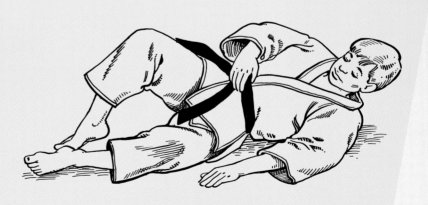

Fall backwards and topple to the left while breaking your fall with your left arm. Slap the mat with your palm to break the impact.

Judo

Throwing

There are 65 recognized throws in judo, and they each have a Japanese and an English name.

Three basic throws allow you to throw your opponent forward, backward, or to the side. Practice the throws at first in slow motion. Then combine the stages into one sequence to develop a smooth action.

Ogoshi—major hip throw

Hip throws, of which there are more than 10, involve using your hip to lift your partner and then rotate him or her over and onto the mat. The major hip throw, called **ogoshi**, helps you learn to use your hip to throw your partner **(uke)** while keeping both feet firmly on the ground.

Grip the uke's sleeve with your left hand, keeping your right arm free.

With a jumping motion, turn your back to the uke with bent legs, as you thrust your arm inside his arm and around his middle. Pull his hips against your back.

Lift the uke over your back as you straighten your legs. Turn the uke flat onto his back and release your grip as he is thrown onto the mat. Bend your legs and help the uke's breakfall with your left arm.

Hand throws

The power of hand throws comes initially from the hands. Once the uke is moving, it is difficult for him or her to stop. The force of your shoulder takes the uke over your shoulder and smoothly down to the mat.

Ippon seoinage—shoulder throw

The shoulder throw takes the **tori** low under the uke. By straightening her knees, leaning forward and twisting, the tori can lift the uke up and over her shoulders. As the tori steps in to attack, he is vulnerable to a counterattack and must be ready to change plans and defend.

The tori sinks his body weight into the uke's chest, limiting the uke's ability to counterattack.

Groundwork

The third broad area of judo technique refers to the point-scoring grapples that take place on the mat. "Hold-downs" involve pinning the uke down on his or her back to score points. The object of groundwork is to position your partner so that he or she is held firmly down on the back for 30 seconds. Juniors are not permitted to use strangling or armlock techniques.

Kesa gatame—the scarf hold

With your right arm around the uke's neck (like a scarf), take hold of his collar. Hold his right hand at the elbow with your left hand. Spread your legs and press your hip against his ribcage.

Press your hip down hard against his trunk and trap his right arm under your armpit to prevent him from twisting free.

As the tori straightens her knees the uke will be lifted off the ground.

Aikido

The training and skills of aikido are different from the other Japanese martial arts. The underlying philosophy of aikido is a strong harmonious development of the mind, the body, and a mysterious force known as **ki**. Ki is a kind of force or power that is believed to be inherent in each human being.

The martial art of aikido seeks to redirect an attacker's strike. Force is not met with counterforce. It is met with an avoiding action, enabling the defender to take advantage of the attacker's temporary loss of balance to score with a successful aikido technique.

Aikido involves redirecting the force of an attacker's blow.

History

The founder of Aikido was a high-ranking ju-jitsu instructor, Morihei Ueshiba. He was severely weakened by scarlet fever as a teenager and turned to the martial art ju-jitsu to build up his strength. Morihei Ueshiba then founded the discipline of aikido or "The Way of Harmony." Professor Toniki played an important role in developing aikido as a sport.

Legend of Morihei Ueshiba

At the age of 85, Ueshiba, who was just 5 feet (150 centimeters) tall and weighed only 110 pounds (50 kilograms), held a demonstration of aikido. He invited six challengers to attack him simultaneously. They did so, and the old man, with barely a visible move, sent his would-be attackers flying in all directions.

To prove the effectiveness of aikido, Morihei Ueshiba had drawn a small chalk circle around his feet. Such little movement was required that he was still within the circle after his assailants had been thrown well clear.

The nage and the uke are assessed according to the fluency and accuracy of each technique in the kata sequence.

Forms of aikido

There are two broad categories of aikido: competitive (**tanto randori**, **randori kyoghi**, and **ninindori**) and noncompetitive (**kata**).

Kata

Kata is noncompetitive aikido. It is a formal display event in which a defender **(nage)** and an attacker **(uke)** display a series of moves of their choice within a time limit of 2 to 3 minutes. Each of the moves must consist of aikido techniques.

The nage and the uke enter the area and bow to the judges. The nage is the person demonstrating the techniques, and the uke takes the falls. They bow to one another from about 13 feet (4 meters) apart and then present their kata. They then return to their original positions, bow to each other, and turn to the judges to await their assessment.

Assessment of the kata display is based on:

- the quality of avoiding attacks
- the quality of breaking the attacker's balance
- correct positioning
- correct execution of moves
- correct posture and movement.

Aikido

Tanto randori

Tanto randori is one of the competitive forms of aikido. It involves the same techniques as **kata** aikido, but is a free-fighting contest fought over two rounds, of 2 minutes each. One competitor, the **uke,** is armed with a rubber knife, while his opponent, the **nage,** is not armed.

To score points the uke must strike the nage's back or front between the belt and shoulders. Each attack must be struck with correct aikido technique from at least one pace away. The attack must also be delivered from the hip, and it must strike the target knife tip first.

If the uke's attack is deflected as it hits the nage, it does not score. One point is scored by the nage for a perfect aikido move or for causing the uke to drop the knife. A successful move with slightly flawed technique scores half a point.

When one fighter scores two points, he or she is immediately declared the winner.

Disarming a knife attack

Randori kyoghi

Randori kyoghi is an unarmed contest of free fighting similar to tanto randori, except that neither competitor has a knife. The contest lasts for 3 minutes, or ends as soon as one contestant scores two points. Points are scored as for a tanto randori match.

As your opponent lifts his or her knee, take up a guard position with your feet apart and your arms outstretched.

Ninindori

Ninindori is a form of competitive aikido fought among three contestants. Contestants take turns being the nage (defender) and fight the other two competitors (uke), for 30 seconds each. The attacks of the uke must begin one step away from the tori; the uke are not permitted to use kicks.

Deflecting a kick

Deflecting an attack is an important technique in any form of aikido.

As your opponent kicks, slide your right foot around and turn so that you avoid the kick. As you move, lift up the kicking leg with your right arm to unbalance your adversary.

Getting Ready

You must warm up and stretch your muscles and joints so that you will not injure yourself when you begin to learn and practice the various martial arts movements. Jog on the spot or walk for 3 to 5 minutes to increase your body temperature and heart rate before stretching.

Neck stretch
Gently pull your head towards your shoulder until you feel the stretch. Hold the stretch for about 10 seconds and then stretch the other side.

Star jumps
Stand with your feet together and your arms by your sides. Jump up and land with your feet apart and your arms outstretched. Then jump back to the start position. Repeat about 15 times.

Hamstring and lower back stretch
Sit on the floor with one leg stretched out straight in front. Your other leg is bent so that your foot touches the knee of your straight leg. Reach toward your toes keeping your back as straight as possible.

Arm circles
Stretch your arms above your head and then take them around in circles, stretching as far up and around as you can. Repeat 10 times forward and 10 times backward.

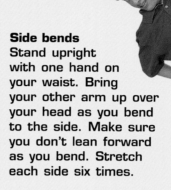

Side bends
Stand upright with one hand on your waist. Bring your other arm up over your head as you bend to the side. Make sure you don't lean forward as you bend. Stretch each side six times.

Lower back stretch
Lie on your back with your legs outstretched. Bend one knee up to your chest and lift your head and shoulders off the floor to meet it. Lower yourself and then stretch the other side. Repeat 10 times.

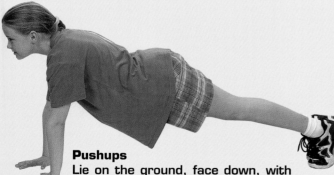

Pushups
Lie on the ground, face down, with your toes tucked under and your hands beside your shoulders. Push up with your arms, keeping your body straight. Then lower your body back to the floor. Repeat 10 times.

Arm and shoulder stretch
Bend your arm behind your head and gently push your elbow down with your other hand.

Taking it Further

United States Martial Arts Association
(USMA)
P.O. Box 18094
Colorado Springs, CO 18094
phone: (719) 635-2976

North American Sport Karate
Asscociation (NASKA)
P.O. Box 581188
Minneapolis, MN 55458-1188
phone: (612) 731-9000
fax: (612) 633-5154

More Books to Read

Armentrout, David. *Martial Arts*. Vero Beach, FL: Rourke Book Company, Inc. 1997.

Casey, Kevin. *Judo*. Vero Beach, FL: Rourke Corporation. 1994.

Dallas, Kim. *Fundamental Karate*. Minneapolis, MN: Lerner Publishing Group. 1998.

Gutman, Bill. *Judo*. Danbury, CT: Children's Press. 1995.

Jensen, Julie. *Beginning Karate*. Minneapolis, MN: The Lerner Publishing Group. 1998.

Mitchell, David. *The Young Martial Arts Enthusiast*. New York: D K Publishing, Inc. 1997.

Nardi, Thomas J. *Karate & Judo*. Chatham, NJ: Raintree Steck-Vaughn. 1996.

Potts, Steve. *Learning Martial Arts*. Danbury, CT: Children's Press. 1996.

Randall, Pamela. *Judo*. New York: Rosen Publishing Group. 1998.

Randall, Pamela. *Aikido*. New York: Rosen Publishing Group. 1998.

Glossary

belt part of the martial arts kit, indicates the performer's level of proficiency

block a defense move that prevents an opponent's punch, strike, or kick from hitting your body

breakfall a technique for falling that allows a martial artist to hit the ground with minimal impact

chudan punches to the target area around the chest

dojo training place or hall where martial arts are practiced

gedan punches to the lower area of the body

gi the training uniform or kit in the martial art of karate

groundwork techniques, such as holds, performed on the mat

ippon full point awarded in competitions when a technique is performed perfectly

jodan punches to the head area

judogi the training uniform or kit in the martial art of judo and aikido

judoka participant in judo

karateka participant in karate

kata a series of set martial arts movements

kesa gatame a judo hold, performed once the opponent has been thrown onto the mat

ki inner strength and energy of the body in aikido

koka a low score in judo

kyu a grade level of karate

nage performer of aikido technique

ninindori aikido contest, where each of three competitors take a turn defending against two opponents

ogoshi a major throw from the hip in judo

randori kyoghi unarmed aikido contest

shobu sanbon hajime the referee's call to start the karate contest

tanto randori aikido contest where one competitor is armed with a rubber knife

tori martial artist performing a move

uke martial artist on the receiving end of a move

waza ari half point awarded in competition when a technique is performed well

yoi stance ready position in karate

yuko a low score in judo

Index